WRITING THE
DECLARATION OF INDEPENDENCE

BY MATT BOWERS

AMICUS | AMICUS INK

Sequence is published by Amicus and Amicus Ink
P.O. Box 1329, Mankato, MN 56002
www.amicuspublishing.us

Library of Congress Cataloging-in-Publication Data
Names: Bowers, Matt, author.
Title: Writing the Declaration of Independence / by Matt Bowers.
Description: Mankato, Minnesota : Amicus, 2020. | Series: Sequence American
  Government | Includes index. | Description based on print version record
  and CIP data provided by publisher; resource not viewed.
Identifiers: LCCN 2018039975 (print) | LCCN 2018042134 (ebook) |
  ISBN 9781681517551 (pdf) | ISBN 9781681516738 (library binding) |
  ISBN 9781681524597 (pbk.)
Subjects: LCSH: United States. Declaration of
  Independence--Chronology--Juvenile literature. | United States--Politics
  and government--1775-1783--Chronology--Juvenile literature.
Classification: LCC E221 (ebook) | LCC E221 .B68 2020 (print) | DDC
  973.3/13--dc23
LC record available at https://lccn.loc.gov/2018039975

Editor: Alissa Thielges
Designer: Veronica Scott
Photo Researcher: Holly Young

Photo Credits: Good Free Photos/John Trumbull cover; WikiCommons cover, 5; iStock/
Nikada 5; Getty/Culture Club 6; WikiCommons/unknown artist 9; AP/North Wind
Picture Archives 10–11; Bridgeman Images/Look and Learn, English School 12–13;
Flickr/WikiCommons/Allyn Cox 14; National Guard/Don Troiani 17; WikiCommons/
National Picture Gallery/Laurent Dabos 18–19; WikiCommons/J.L.G. Ferris 21;
WikiCommons/Rembrandt Peale 22; WikiCommons/John Trumbull 24–25; Alamy/
Album 26–27; Getty/Ariel Skelley 29

Printed in the United States of America

HC 10 9 8 7 6 5 4 3 2 1
PB 10 9 8 7 6 5 4 3 2 1

The Declaration of Independence

On July 4th, cities host parades. They shoot fireworks. Why? It's Independence Day! People are celebrating the birthday of the United States. This is the day the **Declaration** of Independence was **adopted** in 1776. It declared the United States was a new nation. It also separated the American **colonies** from Great Britain's rule.

The Declaration of Independence is celebrated every July 4th.

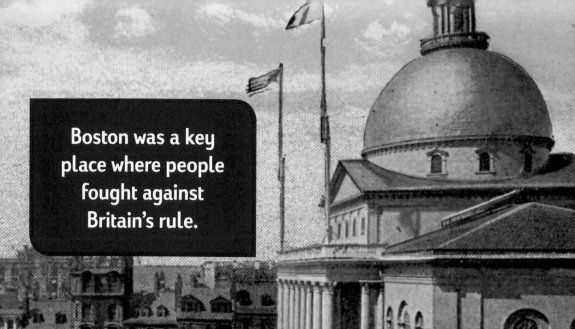

Boston was a key place where people fought against Britain's rule.

Great Britain wins war against France.

1763

LOADING...LOADING...

Trouble in the Colonies

The path to independence was not easy. Trouble was brewing in 1763. Great Britain had just fought a war against France. Britain won. But now it owed a lot of money. To raise the funds, Britain made its American colonies pay **taxes**. Britain thought this was fair. Part of the war had been to protect the colonies.

Britain passed a lot of tax **acts**. The first was the Sugar Act in 1764. This was a tax on sugar and other items. The Stamp Act was passed in 1765. This taxed newspapers, playing cards, and other printed items. In 1767, the Townshend Acts began. More taxes! Now paint, glass, paper, and tea cost more. These taxes made the colonists mad.

Great Britain wins war against France.

1763

1764-1767

DING . . . LOADING . . .

Great Britain passes the Sugar Act, Stamp Act, and Townshend Acts.

People in Boston burn
paper goods taxed by the
Stamp Act.

Great Britain wins war against France.

Five colonists die in the Boston Massacre.

1763   1764-1767   MARCH 5, 1770

. . . L O A D I N G . . .

Great Britain passes the Sugar Act, Stamp Act, and Townshend Acts.

The colonists took action. They **protested**. They did not buy British goods. This worked, and Britain **repealed** a lot of taxes. But on March 5, 1770, there was a fight in Boston. British soldiers fired on the protestors. In the end, five colonists died. More were hurt. This was the Boston Massacre. It made the colonists even more upset.

Colonists fight British soldiers in the Boston Massacre.

The Tea Act was passed in 1773. The colonists could only buy tea from Britain now. This led to a protest called the Boston Tea Party. On December 16, 1773, colonists boarded three British ships in Boston Harbor. They tossed the tea into the sea. They ruined hundreds of chests of tea. Britain was furious. The harbor was closed. Colonists were forced to house British soldiers.

Colonists dressed as American Indians to hide who they were at the Boston Tea Party.

Great Britain wins war against France.

Five colonists die in the Boston Massacre.

1763   1764–1767   MARCH 5, 1770   1773   )ADING . . .

Great Britain passes the Sugar Act, Stamp Act, and Townshend Acts.

Great Britain passes the Tea Act, leading to the Boston Tea Party protest.

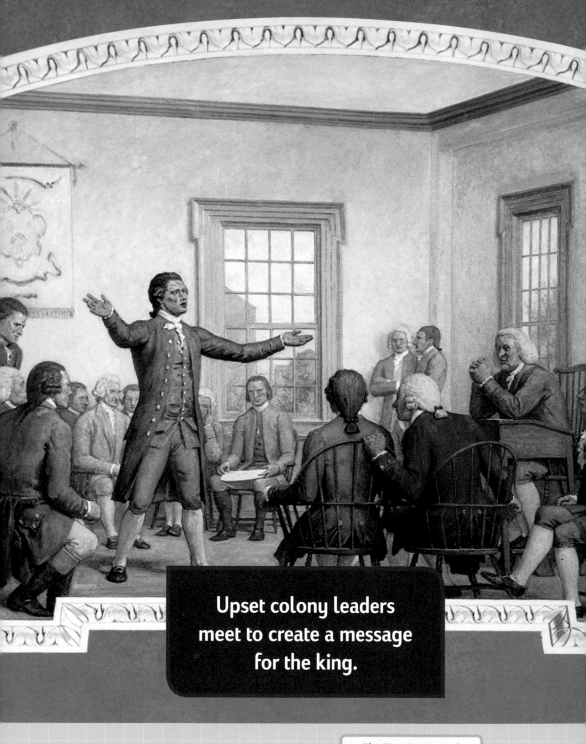

Upset colony leaders meet to create a message for the king.

Great Britain wins war against France.

Five colonists die in the Boston Massacre.

The First Continental Congress meets and sends message to Britain.

1763   1764-1767   MARCH 5, 1770   1773   SEPTEMBER 1774

Great Britain passes the Sugar Act, Stamp Act, and Townshend Acts.

Great Britain passes the Tea Act, leading to the Boston Tea Party protest.

Choosing Independence

In September 1774, leaders from the colonies met in Philadelphia. This was the First Continental Congress. They sent a message to King George III and Britain. It was a list of demands. They didn't want any more British troops.

They asked for an end to all the taxes. They wanted the Boston Harbor to be opened. The colonists had many demands. King George never sent a reply.

Many colonists were still unhappy. Fights broke out. On April 19, 1775, British troops fought a group of colonists in Lexington. This was the start of the Revolutionary War (1775—1783). In early 1776, Thomas Paine published a **pamphlet**. It was called *Common Sense*. In it, Paine gave reasons for American independence.

Great Britain wins war against France.	Five colonists die in the Boston Massacre.	The First Continental Congress meets and sends message to Britain.	
1763	1764-1767	MARCH 5, 1770	1773 SEPTEMBER 1774 JANUARY 1776
	Great Britain passes the Sugar Act, Stamp Act, and Townshend Acts.	Great Britain passes the Tea Act, leading to the Boston Tea Party protest.	Thomas Paine's pamphlet urges split from Britain.

Colonists in Lexington
fire at British soldiers.

LOADING . . . LOADING . . . LOADING . . .

Great Britain wins war against France.

Five colonists die in the Boston Massacre.

The First Continental Congress meets and sends message to Britain.

1763   1764-1767   MARCH 5, 1770   1773   SEPTEMBER 1774   JANUARY 1776

Great Britain passes the Sugar Act, Stamp Act, and Townshend Acts.

Great Britain passes the Tea Act, leading to the Boston Tea Party protest.

Thomas Paine's pamphlet urges split from Britain.

Paine's idea caught on. A lot of people wanted to be free from Britain. But some wanted to stay with Britain. On June 7, 1776, the Second Continental Congress met. Richard Henry Lee was there. He agreed with Paine's bold idea. He said the colonies should declare independence. This was called the Lee **Resolution**.

Thomas Paine's writing inspired Americans to fight to be free of Britain.

Lee Resolution proposes independence from Great Britain.

JUNE 7, 1776

LOADING . . . LOADING . . .

Jefferson Writes the Declaration

Congress needed a document. The colonies would declare their independence from Britain in writing. Five people were chosen to write it. Thomas Jefferson was one of them. The other four chose him. They thought that he was the best writer. He began writing it on June 11, 1776.

Great Britain wins war against France.		Five colonists die in the Boston Massacre.		The First Continental Congress meets and sends message to Britain.	
1763	1764–1767	MARCH 5, 1770	1773	SEPTEMBER 1774	JANUARY 1776
	Great Britain passes the Sugar Act, Stamp Act, and Townshend Acts.		Great Britain passes the Tea Act, leading to the Boston Tea Party protest.		Thomas Paine's pamphlet urges split from Britain.

Benjamin Franklin looks over Jefferson's work on the Declaration.

Lee Resolution proposes independence from Great Britain.

JUNE 7, 1776   JUNE 11, 1776

ING... LOADING...

Thomas Jefferson begins writing a declaration to Britain.

Thomas Jefferson played a key role in shaping the Declaration.

Great Britain wins war against France.

Five colonists die in the Boston Massacre.

The First Continental Congress meets and sends message to Britain.

| 1763 | 1764-1767 | MARCH 5, 1770 | 1773 | SEPTEMBER 1774 | JANUARY 1776 |

Great Britain passes the Sugar Act, Stamp Act, and Townshend Acts.

Great Britain passes the Tea Act, leading to the Boston Tea Party protest.

Thomas Paine's pamphlet urges split from Britain.

Jefferson wanted to get the words right. This was not just a letter to King George III. It was also a message to the other countries. It explained why the colonists wanted independence. It listed their **grievances** against the king and Britain. It stated their rights and presented them as a new nation. Jefferson finished on June 28.

Lee Resolution proposes independence from Great Britain.

Thomas Jefferson finishes writing a draft of the Declaration of Independence.

JUNE 7, 1776   JUNE 11, 1776   JUNE 28, 1776   LOADING . . .

Thomas Jefferson begins writing a declaration to Britain.

On July 2, Congress voted on the Lee Resolution. It was approved. They were going to declare independence. Congress worked on the Declaration next. They tweaked some of the writing. It took two days. On July 4, 1776, the Declaration of Independence was adopted. The colonies were a new nation. The United States of America was born!

Great Britain wins war against France.

Five colonists die in the Boston Massacre.

The First Continental Congress meets and sends message to Britain.

1763   1764-1767   MARCH 5, 1770   1773   SEPTEMBER 1774   JANUARY 1776

Great Britain passes the Sugar Act, Stamp Act, and Townshend Acts.

Great Britain passes the Tea Act, leading to the Boston Tea Party protest.

Thomas Paine's pamphlet urges split from Britain.

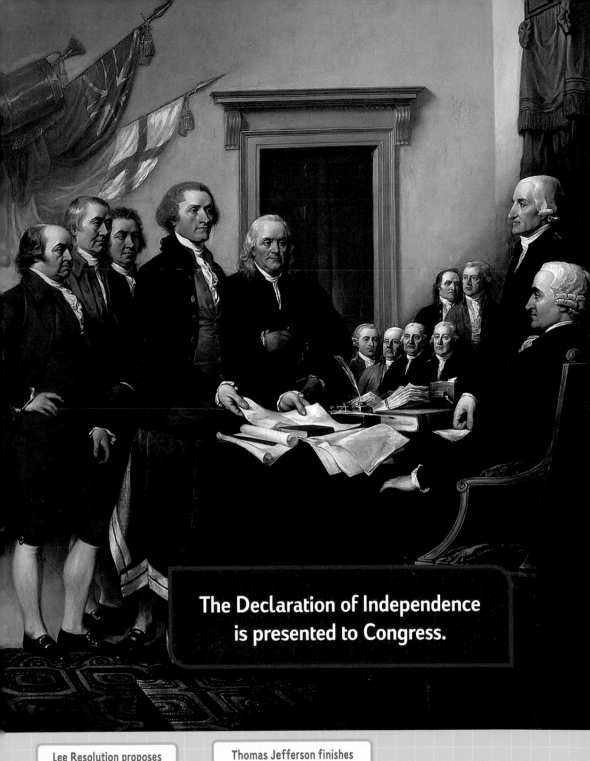

The Declaration of Independence is presented to Congress.

Lee Resolution proposes independence from Great Britain.

Thomas Jefferson finishes writing a draft of the Declaration of Independence.

JUNE 7, 1776   JUNE 11, 1776   JUNE 28, 1776   JULY 4, 1776

Thomas Jefferson begins writing a declaration to Britain.

Congress adopts the Declaration of Independence.

Great Britain wins war
against France.

Five colonists die in the
Boston Massacre.

The First Continental
Congress meets and
sends message to Britain.

1763   1764-1767   MARCH 5, 1770   1773   SEPTEMBER 1774   JANUARY 1776

Great Britain passes the
Sugar Act, Stamp Act, and
Townshend Acts.

Great Britain passes the
Tea Act, leading to the
Boston Tea Party protest.

Thomas Paine's pamphlet
urges split from Britain.

On August 2, Congress signed the Declaration of Independence. This was a special copy, written in ink on **parchment** paper. Signing was a brave thing to do. Britain didn't let the colonies go without a fight. The Revolutionary War went on until 1783. When the war ended, the nation that had begun on July 4, 1776 was free from British rule.

A band celebrates Independence Day during the Revolutionary War.

Lee Resolution proposes independence from Great Britain.

Thomas Jefferson finishes writing a draft of the Declaration of Independence.

The Declaration of Independence is signed.

JUNE 7, 1776   JUNE 11, 1776   JUNE 28, 1776   JULY 4, 1776   AUGUST 2, 1776

Thomas Jefferson begins writing a declaration to Britain.

Congress adopts the Declaration of Independence.

Independence Day Today

Every year, Americans remember the birth of our nation. It all started with the Declaration of Independence. This document is key to American history. Its strong and clear writing explains why we broke free from Great Britain. It also states our rights as humans. It is a **radical** document made in a revolutionary time. And it is what Americans celebrate each year on July 4th.

Great Britain wins war against France.

Five colonists die in the Boston Massacre.

The First Continental Congress meets and sends message to Britain.

| 1763 | 1764-1767 | MARCH 5, 1770 | 1773 | SEPTEMBER 1774 | JANUARY 1776 |

Great Britain passes the Sugar Act, Stamp Act, and Townshend Acts.

Great Britain passes the Tea Act, leading to the Boston Tea Party protest.

Thomas Paine's pamphlet urges split from Britain.

Kids march in a
Fourth of July parade.

Lee Resolution proposes independence from Great Britain.		Thomas Jefferson finishes writing a draft of the Declaration of Independence.		The Declaration of Independence is signed.
JUNE 7, 1776	JUNE 11, 1776	JUNE 28, 1776	JULY 4, 1776	AUGUST 2, 1776
	Thomas Jefferson begins writing a declaration to Britain.		Congress adopts the Declaration of Independence.	

Glossary

act A law made by lawmakers.

adopt To formally approve or accept.

colony A piece of land that has been settled by people from another country and is controlled by that country.

declaration A formal statement or announcement.

grievance A cause of distress (such as extra taxes) that gives people a reason to complain or protest.

pamphlet A small, thin booklet, usually containing information on one particular topic.

parchment Heavy, paper-like material made from the skin of sheep or goats and used for writing on.

protest To object to something strongly and publicly.

radical Very different from the usual or normal.

repeal To officially end a law.

resolution A firm decision to do or not to do something voted on by a group.

tax Extra money charged on goods that supports the government.

Read More

Harris, Michael C. *What is the Declaration of Independence?* New York: Penguin Random House, 2016.

Leavitt, Amie Jane. *The Declaration of Independence in Translation: What It Really Means.* North Mankato, Minn.: Capstone Press, 2018.

Manger, Katherine. *The Declaration of Independence.* New York: Rosen Publishing, 2017.

Websites

History—Declaration of Independence
https://www.history.com/topics/american-revolution/declaration-of-independence/videos#jefferson-writes-declaration-of-independence

PBS | Liberty! The American Revolution
https://www.pbs.org/ktca/liberty/chronicle_philadelphia1776.html

US History—The Declaration of Independence
http://www.ushistory.org/declaration/index.html

Every effort has been made to ensure that these websites are appropriate for children. However, because of the nature of the Internet, it is impossible to guarantee that these sites will remain active indefinitely or that their contents will not be altered.

Index

About the Author

Matt Bowers is a writer and illustrator who lives in Minnesota. When he's not writing or drawing, he enjoys skiing, sailing, and going on adventures with his family. He hopes readers will continue to learn about government and be leaders in their communities.